About the Author

Jason played drums in the independent music scene for over ten years before he went into hospital. He is now in a wheelchair and spends his creative energy writing.

You're Not Dead

Jason Garden

You're Not Dead

Olympia Publishers
London

www.olympiapublishers.com
OLYMPIA PAPERBACK EDITION

ISBN: 978-1-80074-621-3

First Published in 2022

Olympia Publishers
Tallis House
2 Tallis Street
London
EC4Y 0AB
Printed in Great Britain

Dedication

To my friends, my family, and to the memory of Krista Messier

Acknowledgements

Special thanks to Amanda.

-1

The Hero was sick.

His head hurt and his world was spinning. He awoke in his basement feeling lethargic and slow. The stairs to the main floor were narrow, old and daunting. He ascended them as deftly as he could, avoiding steps that were notoriously weak.

There, his mother was already awake and ready to face the day. With a warm smile, she greeted the Hero.

"Good morning, Love! You look like hell!"

Not exactly the first thing he wanted to hear in the early afternoon, but he said nothing and did nothing to discredit the statement.

"Yeah. I was worried about that."

He then poured himself a cup of coffee and sat quietly in the corner. This raised even more alarms for his mother, who instantly started on the motherly tirade of, "Did you get enough sleep? Are you hungry? I know that is your first cup of coffee, but did you want me to ready another? Drink some water."

"I'm fine." He finally mustered, sounding rather defeated.

He stared at the trees and could almost watch their leaves changing to a bright orange colour. He hated this city, but it was quite beautiful in this season. The air was brisk, but not intrusive yet. Grass was still covering the lawns, and the world was covered by a light dew. The sun refracted over every angle that was within view. Pedestrians on the sidewalks had billows of breath hanging from their mouths. The Hero sat in awe at how incredible the world looked. Everything had a yellow hue to it from the light through the leaves.

He did not want to worry his mother, but he had arranged an appointment with his doctor for later that day. At twenty-four, it would be his first venture into a doctor's office as an adult.

The idea excited the Hero. He looked forward to the future where he could, not only look after his own affairs, but execute them with little interference from anyone in his immediate life.

He finished the coffee and got out of his chair. If he left at that moment, he would still be thirty minutes early. That seemed like a good plan.

He ventured towards the vehicle he would take for this stint. The car was exactly what you would expect in a family dwelling. Grey, four doors, cloth seating, nothing exciting. The Hero still loved it. The speakers were decent and could go loud. This was perfect for listening to music at an inappropriate level.

What was he listening to today? He was a manager at a music store and had worked there for nearly a decade at this point. His collection was huge and varied. With that said, he put on Bibio's Ambivelance Avenue very often. It had a fantastic collection of sounds and ideas.

He started to feel cold. That was weird because it was his favourite weather. Sunny, with mild overcast, and a temperature of about 15C. His sweater had seemed like it should have been enough. He put the heaters on high as he started his journey with the hope that he would warm up soon. The chill just would not leave his bones. He visibly shivered behind the wheel as he merged onto the empty road.

Arriving at the doctor's office, the Hero found a seat in the waiting room. The chair was warm and inviting, which is unusual for a doctor's waiting room. There were four rows of chairs, all the same in build: a metal frame with nylon upholstering. They were not for long term use, as the Hero could already feel his feet swelling due to the way the edge of the seat was cutting off circulation at his knees.

"Just a few more minutes, and I'll say my bit, then go back to bed," the Hero muttered under his breath through gritted teeth. His brain felt three sizes too big for his skull. He wanted another coffee.

They called his name and the Hero jumped up with a start. The "few more minutes" they had promised when he walked in had clearly been long enough for the Hero to fall into a light sleep. The Hero was a strange combination of embarrassed and surprised.

"What time was it, anyway?" he proclaimed aloud, not caring if anyone overheard him.

He was escorted into a room and was asked to sit on a bed. It was cold, and there was paper as a kind of guard against infection. The slab was cold, but it was good to sit down.

Why was he feeling this way? He woke up less than two hours ago and was in the waiting room for what felt like forever! He should not be so excited for the embrace of yet another apparatus for sitting.

Finally, the doctor came in. Small world: The Hero went to high school with his daughter. That was far from news, but it is a fact that he never quite got over.

"Hey! How are you? It feels like I have not seen you in forever!" the doctor was short to launch into small talk. He has been the family doctor of the Hero for just shy of twenty years. Some could view him as a part of the family.

He knew the Hero was not a fan of "conventional" medicine, but he took care of himself. He also knew the Hero was usually a bit peppier than he was displaying today.

"Hey, Doc. I feel horrible. My head and throat hurt, and I am all stuffed up." The Hero cried.

"Well, let's see what's wrong with you," the doctor said while preparing a bunch of medical equipment. He did not sound concerned, which the Hero was thankful for.

The doctor slid a light into the Hero's nose. Then his ears, and down his throat. He straightened up, cleared his throat with a cough, and smiled.

"Well, you have the flu. You'll get worse, but you'll get better. I would stress a flu shot, but it's a bit too late. Go home. Sleep. Eat something. Do you need a note? You should not go to work for a bit." There was much relief and a bit of disappointment felt in the Hero's everything. He would have made the appointment earlier if he knew that he would be given a clean bill of health! Yet, he could not help fearing that it felt much worse than what was being let on.

"That's it?" the Hero said as calmly as he could muster. "I'm going to get worse, but I will get better?"

"Yes," the doctor stated bluntly.

They then exchanged pleasantries, and then the Hero was on his way. It all seemed too simple, but he was not going to cause a ruckus. If the Doctor said he was fine, there was no use arguing over it.

The Hero then headed back into his car and started back on the short drive home. He could not get the idea out of his head that things were worse than they appeared.

"Was it really just a flu?" The Hero then pulled into his driveway and went back to bed. If the doctor was right, he could sleep this off.

He has in the past and should not fret so intensely.

Then, the Hero lay down in his bed and simply went to sleep.

1

The Hero awakes from a deep slumber.

He is not in his bed. He actually has no clue where he is. There is an intrusive beeping of monitors and equipment all around him. The room was not black, but it was dark. Lights flashed on machines and noises echoed in the room. He notices a cup of water a few feet from where he lies and thinks how his mouth feels rather dry and the cool liquid would feel fantastic at this time.

He tries to lift his arms: no luck, for some reason. He then tries to call out for someone.

Anyone.

He has no voice. Confused.

Alone.

He cries for what feels like an eternity.

Finally, his mother and father come into frame. Their faces gleaming with joy, tears in the crevices of their faces. This made him cry harder. He tries to ask what happened. He tries to offer some form of condolence. He tries to do pretty much anything to gesture that he is okay.

He is unable to. His arms are paralyzed and he is mute.

Defeated, he closes his eyes again and hopes that either everything changes when he awakes, or that he never comes to consciousness again.

The Hero awakes from the quick bout of

overwhelming reality. He is still confused, but his parents are around him. They explain how he died. They explained that he is physically unable to do anything right now. They show him the tube coming out of the front of his throat and explain that is how it is breathing for him. They try to keep their spirits up, but the Hero can see their confidence faltering in their expression.

They explain that something happened. He got sick. He was asleep for a long time. He died.

Twice.

Now he is back and they were happy. They explained how the medical personnel wanted to pull life support weeks prior, but they refused to let them.

The Hero still just wanted a drink of water.

His parents try to explain the last little bit he almost remembers. Apparently, he contracted some sort of flu and his body reacted by inducing encephalitis.

Encephalitis is where the fluid surrounding the brain collects and crushes parts of the grey matter. In his particular case, it crushed the cerebellum and affected a good portion, if not all, of the major motor and health functions. Primarily, those dealing with limb control, nerve reaction, heart rate, and heat regulation.

In a way, the Hero was lucky. If the swelling had been the frontal cortex, it could have damaged his memory. His personality. It would have destroyed who he was.

Legally, he was a quadriplegic. He has no ability to move his legs or arms. Even the movement of his neck was very difficult, if not impossible. The Hero was unable to swallow.

He dreamed of drinking water but was then informed

that he would most likely choke. Even the movements of his tongue could be fatal.

That is when the Hero noticed all of the metal. He counted four long bits of medical steel jutting from each of his forearms. They punctured on the perfect angles to avoid nerves, so they did not hurt. Maybe he could not feel them, anyway.

The Hero was not new to the idea of metal piercing skin. He had received over fifteen piercings in his life: something he was quite proud of. It was a kind of identity for him.

Everyone was the same, but he had shit in his face.

Enter the health care professional. They just came in to check the Hero's vitals and breathing machine. They were surprised that he was as responsive as he was and started immediately asking a million questions. That was when the Hero wanted, but was unable, to move his middle finger to gesture them on their way.

They left, eventually, and immediately the Hero started crying again.

The Hero was an hour from home, laying in Toronto Western Hospital. He remembered that he was somewhat close to people he knew. He wondered if they would know where he was or what state he was in. The door burst open at that point, and Luka ran in.

Luka was the Hero's greatest and longest friend. She had lived in Toronto for a number of years at this point, and the Hero had attempted to make it out to see her and her dog at least once a week before he wound up in hospital.

He was ecstatic to see her and tried his best to put a

smile and a brave face on. She took one look at him and immediately burst into tears of celebration.

It turns out that she was informed the Hero had died about three months before this day. Then, she discovered that he was alive not a month later: close to death, but also down the road. She had been there most days, talking to the unresponsive body. Wishing him back to reality. She told him over and over again how she couldn't bare life without him. When he was informed of all of this, he cried again.

He felt pathetic: crying three times in, what he assumed was, one day. He was just so happy to see her. He was just so happy to be able to see everyone.

Luka hugged him.

He tried as hard as he could to hug back.

He tried to call her a fool for thinking he was gone.

He tried many things.

Luka was nowhere near the only visitor that the Hero was happy to see. While in a coma, he had apparently shut down the main waiting room with all of the people clambering to see him for, what they had believed to be, the last time.

That is when the Hero discovered that the idea had gotten around that he had died. Many people came to pay their respects to him, and his family. When it was reported that he, in fact, did not die: more people came around out of celebration. Benefit concerts that would be held in his memory were simply forgotten due to redundancy.

A great percentage of the people that the Hero had touched came out to wish him well: to remind him just how much he meant to them.

It was January.

The month was even lonelier than usual. People popped in and out of existence all the time, and the Hero would live, for what seemed like, days.

Alone.

In reality, it was just a few hours. Time drags on and on when you are in a hospital. Even the sweet embrace of sleep would not save the Hero feeling truly alone. He spent a lot of time imagining fantastical worlds.

In one such daydream; he was a hunter. He would venture out of his holdings to find rare and mystical beasts to kill them, justly. He remembered vividly thanking them before he ate them. He was a decent chef, but he would cringe when biting into the meat he prepared. A cool breeze would float between the sea of green leaves and across his face.

Once, while he slept, he dreamt that he was flying through the skies. Observing the world around him, drifting between trees and hills. He saw valleys that were coated in green grass, clouds as large as he could picture, and mountains that were red and towering. His speed never held much concern, for the air around him was always warm. He never got lost, for there was no destination. On occasion, his arms were massive wings. Twice the size probably needed to hold one human. He rarely landed, and simply got sustenance while soaring around in the clouds.

The dreams reminded him a lot of what life was. He felt like life was just a series of events not narrated by anyone or anything. Everything happened by accident. All you could do was learn from an experience and move on.

Then he would wake. It was still a jarring resurrection. It often involved tears and frustration. When the dreams ended, he would have to face a version of reality that he did not want. He wanted to escape into that world that he was just in and get lost in it forever. He knew it would be an end, but that did not bother him. He just did not want to find that end.

The nurses would come in. Check vitals. Talk at him (never to him). Leave the room. This was a fate worse than death, he would think. At least if he was dead...

Oh; at least if he was dead.

Bad days seemed so trivial before. He would forget something important, do something stupid, or say something regretful.

Now, bad days were because his body would not let him do what he wants to do. Now, bad days were because he felt trapped. Now, he could not even escape to his old stand-by of driving for a great distance to avoid life. Before, he could leave if he got upset by someone's arrogance or crude depiction of the world. He never saw himself as super intelligent, but he regarded himself as extremely openminded and he was always willing to do research to elaborate on topics he was uneducated about. He had to accept what was around him. He had to endure the oppressive hate and malice that the world contained.

People pretended to be understanding about his condition, and the Hero could sense this. They would put on a brave face, say things that they thought were politically correct, and carry on with their interpersonal relationships.

The Hero could see through all of this. He knew that

people were frightened, that they were curious how this would affect their life. Even his parents, who were nothing but supportive, were concerned about how their life would change. How he changed their life.

It was, after all, his fault.

2

On the ninth of February, the Hero ventured into the world for his first time since the end of October the year before. He was brought to an aquarium about twenty minutes from the hospital. He was placed into a wheelchair, hooked up with oxygen, and had several IV bags.

Oh, what a spectacle he must have been to the uneducated! A collection of flesh surrounded by machines and tubes. He could not help but speculate that they assumed that he was victim of some sort of accident.

They would be as clueless as him. No one had told him, definitively, what happened.

And they probably never would...

He had an exorbitant amount of medical equipment with him. He was also joined by a registered nurse, his mother and his brother.

What an excellent state he was in for his first public outing! More machine than man. This was also his first time being in the public eye since he had turned a quarter century.

It goes without saying that this was not what he had imagined for himself four months prior.

The aquarium was amazing!

He saw aquatic beings the size of homes. He got to touch Manta Rays.

He got a stuffed toy and a cup. It felt like a

consolation prize for living through the day, but it still brought a smile across his face.

That event also marked the beginning of the end of the Toronto part of his adventure. He had been in the same place for four months, only two of which he had even the mildest recollection of. Even though this hospital was the place that saved his life time and time again, it would be foolish to imagine that he would be there forever.

Home.

He was going home. Kind of.

He was going back to the city he grew up in, at the very least. At that point, they were unsure for how long or even what he would be doing when he got there. He still could not move, speak, or swallow. Nutrition was still administered through a syringe. Communication was a combination of blinks and attempted groans. A machine still passed oxygen though his body.

The next note-worthy adventure would be travelling between hospitals. They arranged for a medical transfer which required a vehicle similar to an Ambulance. He was strapped to a cot, because he was still unable to sit erect long enough for the trip. His view for the next hour or so would be the ceiling of a metal coffin.

The journey felt like it took ages. He was alone in the vehicle. He tried to think of something good, anything good, to escape the crushing isolation he was experiencing.

There is something to be said about silence, relative stillness, and isolation when you have been run ragged by the times at hand.

He had been, however, in relative isolation for almost

five months at this point.

There was still an annoying noise resonating from the machines that helped him to breathe and the roar of the road under the tires. He was a drummer: he noticed when the sounds were not in beat. It sounds petty, but he was aware of it, and could not ignore it no matter how hard he tried. He was unable to find even a mild syncopation between the bumps and drops in the road and the constant meter held by the breathing machine.

The breathing machine.

That horrible, heavy assistant to his life. He knows that, without it, he would be dead. It does not mean that he likes it. Quite the opposite: there was a sense of unwanted dependency that has become apparent to him. He knew he owed his life to that thing, but he hated it so much.

Was he suicidal? No. Did he wish he died? Yes. His life was not fantastic before this point. He worked an entry level job that he was comfortable being in because it was easy. He played in the local music scene with little success and stubbornly held onto the idea that he could survive on nothing more than dreams. He had wronged a good portion of people in his life by either promises that he never came through on or he betrayed them. So many things that built up to make days just bearable until his next adventure but...

...this was a whole new low. Since he was lying down, he was not able to see where he was going. He just stared at the cold metal casing that would move him from one city to another. He was still strapped into oxygen and still had a plethora of IVs and monitors. He was too far away from the nurse and driver who also occupied the vehicle, or he would have asked what everything he was hooked up to was for. Call it morbid, but he wanted to know, not just speculate, what all the tubes were doing. He wanted to ask so many questions, but he could not even produce a heavy sigh.

Maybe it was for the best that he was alone.

***

The arrival back in Cambridge was without fanfare or celebration. The administration was completed by the Hero's parents while he was whisked away to a room. Within an hour of him being placed into a bed, there was a massive collection of doctors and nurses all being briefed on what the situation could be.

They were all given tasks and goals and dispersed almost as fast as they had gathered. For the Hero, it was all painless. He was, by all definition, mute. Any questions about treatment or pain were answered by speculation, clipboards and charts. Plans were drawn up immediately for new treatments and plans were executed without input from anyone, and execution started quickly.

Today was they day the hospital wanted to try to remove the breathing tube from the Hero. He was nervous. As much as he hated the tube coming out of the front of his neck, there was comfort in it. He knew that as long as it was there, he could breathe. He knew that when it was removed, he would have a very evident and very prominent scar.

He felt very vain thinking about how the removal of something like that would affect his appearance, but he had already lost 15 piercings through this ordeal. He felt out of control of his identity and worried that he would have little say in how things went forward.

He had to wonder if it was unnecessary to focus on how little input he had in his appearance with everything he had gone through. Maybe he should be focused on how his life will change. He could not fathom how different life would be, but he knew that he wanted to look his best. He could not express himself in audible tones, so the very least he wanted was to have a kind of say in his appearance.

The tube coming out was the worst thing, arguably, that he had experienced since he regained consciousness. It was a long process over the period of a week.

First, the medical staff would remove the tube for an hour and put a kind of cork in the esophagus. This would force him to breath in the conventional sense. This would take some level of training.

Breathing should be natural, but the Hero had not done this process for months at this time.

For that hour, the Hero felt like he was drowning above water. For that hour, the Hero wondered who was strangling him.

For that hour, the Hero wanted death.

This process continued over the next week. Some days he would go half an hour, some days he went several hours as doctors pushed his body further and further. Some days the cork would be in place properly, some days the Hero could feel it slipping out of his windpipe.

The worst for the Hero was when they would put the cork in place and ask him to swallow. Always just water, but it did not go well on occasion. They would force him to sit upright, he would take a sip. The muscles in his mouth were so weak, sometimes it would go right and he would get to feel the fantastic elixir to his stomach. More often, however, his mouth would betray his trust. When that happened, the water would try to go to his lungs. He would cough and sputter. Being too weak to do anything himself, someone would have to bring his head forward as he tried, with everything he had, to try to get the liquid out of his throat so he did not drown.

3

Cambridge.

The Hero spent the majority of his life loafing around the centres of that city, and he loathed that place very much.

It was horribly arrogant and had little reason to be.

Oh: it was pretty. It was at the intersection of two rivers, and forests lined the banks of the water. That was, however, being destroyed in attempts to make everything more commercial. More "convenient" for residents and tourists alike.

Forests were destroyed at a rapid pace. Rivers were exploited for their eye-candy, and ironically treated horribly during their exploitation.

He was brought into Cambridge Memorial Hospital. It was explained to him that this was his second time inside that building since his journey started. He cannot remember the first time.

He finds that haunting - wrong almost. He feels like the month before he fell into a coma was narrated by someone else, but he still acted out the conclusions of his actions. He was left to wonder: did he really mean everything his husk did?

The first room he was placed into was a grand size (or at least he thought it was). He had two other roommates, which was something he was not accustomed to. He had been kept in solitary rooms until this point in his journey.

They kept to themselves. He never did hear much regarding their stories.

The one guy was about ten years the Hero's senior. He seemed very sick and was quarantined several times in the week they shared that room. The other gentleman was much older: probably in his 60s. The younger gentleman had a few visitors, mostly friends and family, that seemed to come on an almost daily schedule. The older patron had, what the Hero assumed, a wife that came when she could. She came out to be a healthy amount, but the man was left alone more often than not.

There was a sense that whatever the older man was in the hospital for was acute and he would be out in time. The Hero had the feeling it would not be to his house, but at least back into society.

Not so much with the other gentleman. The Hero wished he knew what was wrong. He was under quarantine most of the time.

This was all just speculation made by the Hero, however.

The nursing staff was horrible. They were clearly overworked. Or they were just incredibly apathetic.

Or they were just horribly stupid.

One such nurse seemed to mean well but would just say and do all the wrong things.

The Hero was reminded of that person who would be in your high school class that, no matter how right or wrong she was, you would just cringe with every noise she made. She would always speak to everyone else in the room and talk to the Hero as if he was a child.

He wanted to tell her off. He wanted to remind her that

he was human.

He still could not speak.

The Hero was visited several times by his friends Shannon and Ryan. He loved them both very much and was glad every time he saw their faces. They would crack jokes at everything they could and kept everyone in good spirits. Shannon, in particular, has been a friend of the family for many years. Her presence was greatly appreciated by the present company.

During one visit from the pair, the Nasal Gastric tube that was in the Hero was bothering him.

A Nasal Gastric tube is a tube that travels through a nose, down a throat, and creates a clear path between a face and a stomach. It is used to administer medications and some paste that is meant to pass for food.

It was annoying and obstructive. There was a chance that, if he got food into his mouth somehow, he would choke and die.

The Hero still did not have movement in any part of his arms. So, in pathetic attempts and whimpers, he gestured towards removing it. The nurse he did not like refused on multiple occasions.

"It's necessary." She would harp without further explanation. This statement was usually followed by a sharp turn to anyone else and disregard for any further attempt at communication made by the Hero.

The Hero hated her so much.

Shannon noticed how uncomfortable the tube made the Hero immediately. Carefully, she removed it. The Hero could feel the plastic rubbing against the inside of his throat, which was mildly uncomfortable. The hated nurse stood and watched as the tube came out.

She waited for the tube to be fully removed before making her presence known.

"WHAT ARE YOU DOING?!" The nurse shrieked as loud as she could. It was piercing. "DO YOU KNOW WHAT YOU HAVE DONE?!"

She ripped the tube from Shannon's hand and grumbled as she left the room. Funnily enough, the Hero never saw her after that. He hoped that event caused some sort of hammer to be brought from on high to get her in trouble. He kept wishing she would just stick her head in and apologize so he could refuse her existence entirely, but he never wanted to see her again.

The Hero was moved around the hospital often. He had a constant worry that something would vanish, and stuff did, but nothing important ever got left behind.

He did lose a stuffed toy that his friends Chrissy and Adam had given him. It was a Narwhal. He was fantastic, and the Hero was not above admitting that. Yes, it was juvenile, but he breathed through a machine. The Hero doubted that anyone would give him a hard time right now.

The exact time or place that went missing is unknown. The Hero assumed that it had been gone since he left Toronto.

The hospital in Cambridge, though close to friends and family, was lonelier than his solitary room in Toronto. The fanfare of his survival has subsided, and he was reduced to spending much of his time alone.

To be clear, he did have a few visitors, but not as many as he would have liked.

He felt selfish. He knew that it must have been far from entertaining to talk to a lifeless lump, but he still wanted someone to talk at him. Yet, day after day, he was left alone with nothing interrupting all of his thoughts.

***

The medical staff decided that he needed what they referred to as a "PLEX" about a week or two days or a few hours after he got there.

PLEX is the removal of the Plasma from his blood followed by its reintroduction within seconds. It is kind of like a blood transfusion mixed with a blood cleaning. The Hero did not quite understand, but he was in no position to object.

Another needle: after what the Hero had been through, he was far from afraid.

He should have been.

He still did not know his age and barely knew his name.

On a winter afternoon, or day, or night, or morning, the Hero was wheeled across the hospital. It was quiet, and the wing he was brought to was relatively empty. He was deposited into a room where he waited for the specialist.

The Hero was in and out of consciousness during the whole ordeal. After all was said and done, he was assured that he had missed little, but the following he remembered all too well.

The PLEX required a major artery. They went through the Hero's jugular. For the uneducated, that is the major artery in the neck.

33

Surprise!

The Hero had feeling there.

He really wished he did not have feeling there.

After the piercing of flesh, the machine turned on. Out of view of the Hero, the machine made stereotypical machine sounds: a constant buzzing and whirling permeated the room with a great weight and volume.

The needle hurt. Even after all of his piercings and two tattoos, the needle was the worst pain the Hero had ever felt. That time he broke his ankle was preferable to this. It was probably not five inches long, but you could have fooled him.

There was a sharp sting as they pierced the flesh in his neck. He stayed conscious, but just barely. Everyone involved looked incredibly bored, like it was just another day at the office.

The nurses, who were normally smiling, had faces of stone. His mother could do nothing but hold his hand and reassure him that everything would be over soon. His brother remained stoic in the corner of the room.

He was completely unaware of how long the procedure actually took, but it felt like an eon.

People swear the room was well lit. It was in a hospital, and they have very sterile lights that light the corners with uniform persuasion.

He remembered it as a dull grey room full of hate, despair and pain.

The sounds from the machine coupled with the long shaft of metal in his neck probably altered his view on the situation slightly.

"Why me? Why now?" He thought to himself while

trying to distract himself from the pain. The whole thing was horrible. He wanted to scream out. All he could manage was darting eyes from corner to corner of the ceiling while tears were streaming from his eyes.

This was horrible.

He already had a blood transfusion back in Toronto. Apparently, he has a very rare blood type for no good reason. His mother is A+. His father is A-. His brother is A+. The Hero, for some reason, is O-. Less than 7% of the world population is O-.

The first donation of blood came to him because that night, a man had died in a motor vehicle accident. Not ideal, but it came at the eleventh hour, apparently. He was in the coma at the time and heard the story from a doctor who was having a particularly bad day. The blood donation involved with the "PLEX" came in a similar fashion: someone's death.

Now, he could claim to be a new man and mean it! He had died twice, he had the blood of at least two other people in his veins. This came with new responsibilities, however. Now, he felt the burden, of not only being the best he can be for him, but of also the best for everyone involved in his life. He was given a second and third chance.

Finally, the machine wound down, the needle was removed, and he was set free. The nurses moved the Hero from where they were doing the operation back to his room. Luckily for him, his bed had wheels. This meant that he never had to try to hobble down halls or be awkwardly placed into a wheelchair. He could not help but feel a twisted sense relief in this situation.

Back to his corner of the world, surrounded by a thin curtain. He laughed at its existence. It was supposed to somehow guard against infectious diseases and viruses. The Hero could make shapes of people out through the pale-yellow veil it cast in the room. The curtains did nothing to inhibit light from outside gracing the corners of his bed.

It was around this time that he was fitted with a (temporary) wheelchair.

Hospital grade, it gave him some sort of mobility. He still could not move his arms, legs, or neck.

He still could not speak.

The Hero still did not know what was actually going on, even though he had heard the stories, and every time he has to remember they are about him.

4

When the Hero was growing up, there was a building up on a hill that he was always curious about. It was large, much like a mansion you would see in old pictures or period films. He never knew what it was, but he assumed it was some sort of government building or office.

Luckily, and unbeknownst to him; it was the destination.

It was a rehab facility called Freeport. The building was up on top of a hill, surrounded by forests and train tracks. This position kept it very isolated from the rest of civilization, in a good way. It was beautiful, for what it was. The low rumble of the freeway was still audible from the grounds, but the view from windows was breathtaking.

The inside of Freeport was four floors. Very well kept. Very clean. It used natural light when it could. This made it look like an old picture or a model found in an attic.

The best part was a fish tank right by a set of doors that lead outside. The Hero felt like an old man. He would park his wheelchair in front of the glass and watch the fish for hours.

Really, the Hero wishes that he was able to enjoy this facility under other circumstances. There was no point to be healthy here, unless you were visiting someone, or this is where you worked.

The main floor is full of shops and administration

rooms. The second floor is spinal issues, third is cancer and other permanent conditions while the fourth is children who were dying of various illnesses. The building was beautiful, but far from happy.

The nurses were friendly here. The Hero did not talk to many of them, but his interactions were pleasant whenever he did. He spent a lot more time interacting with the various therapists on the floor.

He still could not speak. His conversations were little more than eye gestures.

It was great: he had many friends who came out to see him here. It was right in the middle of several areas where they all lived and was quite accessible from everywhere. This meant that he would have friends and loved ones dropping by very often. They would mostly talk at the Hero, for his responses were little more than inappropriate hand gesture attempts and angry facial expressions.

One such day, while a few of his friends were around, the Hero was laughing as heartily as he could.

Suddenly, he did it.

He told his friend, in a loving manor, to "fuck himself".

His first words.

The first he spoke in over three months were inappropriate and glorious.

It shocked everyone nearby.

"Was… was that… me?" The Hero whispered.

Tears erupted from every angle. The Hero was beside himself with disbelief, and his friends were no better. For as hysterical seeming that everyone was, the look of joy on every face was staggering. Nurses and Therapists ran in to make sure everyone was all right and were immediately humbled by the outpour of excitement and joy being expressed.

The Hero was asked all sorts of questions. "What was it like to die?"

"Do you remember anything?"

"What can you and can't you feel?"

He tried to answer every question, but his voice was little more than a whisper. Tears still stained his face. As happy as the Hero was, he was angry. Now he could express that better. There was no stopping him now from going on tirades. Oh, the things he wanted to say!

Then, sleep.

Pretty much mid thought, the Hero passed out. Maybe the excitement got to him? Maybe he was just exhausted from using his voice for the first time in months? Even he would not be sure when he finally gained consciousness over fourteen hours later.

The room was still black. Late winter mornings are very isolating.

The Hero was alone, and he did not know why again.

***

The Hero had a roommate. His name was John, and John was much older than the Hero: forty years older, give or take. He was a harsh man. He made his opinions known. He was loud and he would get very angry if things did not go the way he wanted them to. He did not give the Hero much time but was always friendly enough whenever he did.

John liked to listen to sports on the radio pretty well all of the time. It was rather annoying to the Hero. It was totally lost on him, as the Hero did not care about sports. Not in a malicious way, it was just never his forte.

He was not at this facility long, either. Maybe ten days, and he was off to a new adventure. This time, he would be going to Hamilton, Ontario: less than an hour away. Now, able to speak, he was ready to express himself.

It is hard to fathom, not being able to express any emotion or thought outside of depression and despair. The Hero was still paralyzed pretty well everywhere. He finally could speak, but he still could not make rude gestures with his hands the way he would like, or even refuse something without whispering and hoping that people understand him. Luckily, he was not faced with many choices yet, and everything was taken care of for him. Much like how a parent would do things for a young child.

Here he was, twenty-five and having people help him to get dressed in the morning. It was horribly demeaning and incredibly awkward. It was only one event of many that the Hero did not like, but it will stick with him for a very long time.

5

Another patient transfer across hills and valleys. This time, the Hero was traveling to the far away land of Hamilton, Ontario. The Hero had recorded an album there long ago and had very little to say that would be considered nice. The city was tired. It had a couple major factories that probably contributed half of the country's pollution, one of the only high security prisons in the region and holds the prize of being the only city where the Hero was offered Heroin upon one of his first visits.

The positives? It had one of the most fantastic views in the country. The escarpment (or lovingly called "The Mountain" by locals) provided many jaw-dropping views of the entire city. Hamilton also could brag about having one of the best art scenes in all of South-Western Ontario. The Hero had played many concerts there just a couple of years prior, and two of his close friends had entrenched themselves deep in the local Punk community.

He would be going to a rehab facility located directly across the road from the aforementioned prison. Sure: there was always the risk of an "undesirable" stumbling over, but the way the sun reflected off the chicken wire was absolutely stunning!

Again, he was transferred in a lying position. He should be getting used to this, but he always felt like he was missing something amazing.

He used to love the drive to Hamilton, even if he did loathe the city. The journey up was beautiful: farms and old buildings littered the countryside between the regions. Fields and fences separated by rocks and small forests. That does not even bring the plethora of random animals into the mix.

The Hero liked barn-yard animals.

All in all, the trip took about an hour, maybe a little less. The driver and two nurses then wheeled the Hero into the room that would be his home for the next several months.

He was examined almost right away. It was confusing for the Hero, as he still did not know quite where he was. Doctors looked him over, checked his charts, then looked him over again. It turns out, because of the coma followed by paralysis, the Hero had developed quite the pressure sore in his coccyx region.

A pressure sore is deterioration of tissue due to an extended bit of, well, pressure being put on an isolated area with no chance of breathing.

The coccyx region is the area of flesh at the base of the spine, right at the tail bone.

Basically: top of the butt crack.

Since the Hero was lying on his back for literal months, one had formed. It was deep enough that you could see his spine and, if you wanted to do something gross, you could fit a whole finger in there.

Just what I fucking needed. Thought the Hero as nurses and doctors swarmed around his butt deciding what to do next. It had been five months, and the Hero was getting very sick of his entire medical adventure.

The Hero was then introduced to the whole nursing staff on shift that day. They seemed like a lovely bunch of people, and much closer in age to him. Not that the Hero had anything against the older generation. He was just finding it very hard to relate, in any capacity, to people that were close to twice his age. In this place, most of the nurses were within ten years of him. This made him happy and more comfortable.

He then met his roommate, Paul.

Paul was a very lovely, and very rude, British gentleman. He is not one to bite his tongue and took great pride in being able to make people smile at very inappropriate things. He had damaged a spot in his spine while doing housework. It had left him paralyzed from the waist down.

Mary, Paul's wife, was in the room as often as she could be. Together, they went out of their way to make the Hero feel welcomed after the dust settled and everyone returned to their shift.

Shortly after the fiasco of settling, the Hero's parents showed up. The Hero could feel nothing but guilt, like he had forced them to travel the hour from home. Luckily, it was a beautiful day. The sun was out, the temperature was quite pleasant. There was little to no wind. It was picturesque.

The Hero was set up with a time-table for daily activities. Physio (or Physical Therapy) twice a day, and Occupational Therapy between these sessions. At this point, however, the Hero just wanted to know when dinner was he was starving. He had left Freeport right around lunch and got to Hamilton just after, so he was ready to consume something.

Alas, he was told he had to wait a few hours for the kitchen staff to prepare the next event.

He took this time to get to know Paul and Mary, and to make sure his parents had had a good ride over. Paul and Mary were natives to Hamilton, which meant that Mary would be in the area if the Hero ever needed anything.

Finally, dinner time. The dining hall was just a big room with rows upon rows of temporary tables. Far from the lap of luxury, but it worked. There we not many chairs; most of the patrons were in wheelchairs. Traditional seating would have made everything cumbersome and awkward.

The Hero got everything on the menu and was horribly disappointed.

It was pork. They said it was pork. It was tough, rubbery, incredibly thin, and just wrong. The vegetables that the Hero ordered were soggy and depressed-looking. The peas were hard. For someone with little motor-control of their arms, it was difficult for the Hero. He did it himself, but barely.

Then he went back to his room and his parents went home. It was a very underwhelming first day at a new place. For the staff and patients, it was business as usual. For him, it was an adventure into the unknown.

There was a machine on a track with a nylon restraint that came down to a bar. It had three hooks to attach to a sling that would be placed under the patient. The machine would then lift the patient high enough that they could be placed into bed without manual lifting. The purpose for such a device was to assist those who could not bear weight at all.

It was like a ride. A very uncomfortable ride.

The beds were comfortable enough if you do not mind sleeping on and in plastic. The nurse came around with the nightly medication. The Hero was just taking the same things that anyone else would: vitamins and supplements. He was very proud of the fact that he did not need anti-inflammatories, pain killers, or anything of that nature.

Maybe pride was the wrong emotion to feel. "Lucky." That is a better way of putting it.

There was one pill that the Hero had never taken before. It was a sleeping aid. He was sceptical that something that small could help him sleep at all. He figured that it was safe: it was, at all, being offered in a hospital. He scoffed at the notion that he was offered a half. How could half of something so small be enough to render him unconscious?

He was asleep within fifteen minutes.

6

Waking up to nurses scurrying around will never be comfortable to the Hero. They try, so very hard, to not be disruptive. Yet, try as they might, anyone not deep in slumber will be awoken to their motions.

In this case, it was a nurse hovering over the foot of the Hero's bed. She was checking his bags of life juice. He was not mad, but still glared at her. He could not help it.

He was having a magical dream where he was running around a music festival. In his dream, he knew that he would be performing soon. In his dream, he was advertising a new album that was available to the interested. In his dream, it was life as normal, with no horrors of reality, or at least his current reality.

That is one thing that the Hero took great pride in: he never had dreams about being sick or in a wheelchair. He saw the wheelchair being a part of his subconscious as an acceptance of where he was. He saw dreaming of such a thing as a kind of an endgame. That was a concept that he kept to himself for a very long time.

Today was as exciting as any of this had been. Due to his condition, they borrowed him an electric wheelchair. The Hero felt like a boss. It was huge, but quiet.

The Hero sat roughly at the height of 5'2" in the chair. The seat was on top of an electric motor which was attached to a joystick. There were six tires: four larger ones for motion, and two smaller for direction. The difference between them was mostly ignorable, as they just were a few centimetres in size different from each other. There was a slider between two different speed settings: Rabbit and Turtle. The animations to signify the two were simple, yet adorable.

This new chair gave a freedom to the Hero that he craved. No longer did he have to rely on others to move him from point to point. The controls were simple enough that he was accustomed to driving within a few moments.

He liked Turtle mode.

After the day-two introduction, they brought him breakfast to his bed. The Hero was excited. They offered breakfast at Freeport, but he was forced to go to a dining hall to get it.

Wow. I am complaining about that.

In his defence, he was in a manual wheelchair then without even the ability to feed himself. Over the week, he had regained a lot of his strength. He still could not move himself in a manual wheelchair, but he could mostly feed himself, kind of.

After the nurse left and breakfast was consumed, he was left alone with his roommate for the first time since he got there the day before. The Hero and Paul had a few hours before Physiotherapy, so it was time to converse, time to get to know the other entity in the room.

Paul was born in England. He was married to Mary, who was older than he. He had worked as a landscaper for a while. Doing work on some pipes in his bathroom, he had twisted and done something weird to his spine. He had been in hospital for a month at that point, living in the same room for "too long". Paul was in a manual wheelchair and was quite deft at motions in said chair.

Their introductions were cut short when the nurse came to put the Hero in his chair. The lift thing was fun. The Hero was afraid, at first, but it did not take long and he forgot his fears. It felt like a very slow rollercoaster. The reality, however, was that it was more like a ski lift: slow, gentle, and out of necessity.

"Wheee!" The Hero exclaimed, as his body was moved from bed to chair. The nurse just rolled her eyes and smiled to herself.

Up for the first time in over twenty-four hours, given relative freedom for the first time in five months: what is the first thing the Hero would do?

Find a window and look out it.

PLANS!

The Hero realized that it was a simple pleasure, but one his has not partaken in for quite some time. It was magnificent.

It was ten. The sun had risen a few hours earlier, and light penetrated the leaves to produce pale shadows on the earth. There was a slight breeze, but overall, it looked very hot out there. Based on what the Hero had heard, it was the warmest March in several years.

The Hero moved away from the window and proceeded out the door. This was a new adventure for him; new halls and destinations awaited him. Out the door, he noticed that it was a ghost town at that time around the facility. There were empty showers across the way, and his room was in the middle of two others, but no one was nearby to say good morning to.

The Hero felt happy for the first time in months. He was on his own an hour from anyone he knew. He did not feel any judgement or pressure. He was not made to feel like he was being pitied. The Hero knew that it was not the intent of his family or friends, but they would show it in their face. Their eyes would be full of tears as they asked how he was. There was very clear intention about not talking about the very recent past. The Hero had many questions, yes, but he was tired of getting half answers. He was tired of being called a miracle. He was tired of hearing about how he should have died.

Suddenly, a wave of panic. He just realized that he had to make his way over to somewhere else to start physiotherapy.

It was explained to him that physiotherapy was like going to the gym. The classes were structured around trying to get the body back up to strength. The main purpose was to ensure that muscles would not become atrophied and bones would not deteriorate.

The Hero had lost almost half of his muscle mass by this point. He was the smallest that he had been in a very long time, and this caused him almost as much grief as not being able to walk did.

He arrived to find a very busy room. There were people everywhere doing some form of exercise. There was a line for the parallel bars and a large group of people gathered to try to outdo one another with weights. Paul was right behind the Hero.

"Out of my way!" He barked. 'Physio' was his favourite part of the day.

The Hero came back to reality and noticed that one of

the therapists had come up to him.

"Hi! I'm Michelle! Let's get to doing stuff!"

Still taken back, the Hero let Michelle take control of his chair, and bring him over to a large machine.

It was a universal weight machine. The part Michelle wanted the Hero to do was just a simple pulling exercise. The Hero was very interested. He still had little to no movement in his arms, but he knew that working them out would increase recovery ten-fold. The Hero was then fitted with gloves that were fastened with Velcro strips. They had a ring for the machine to attach to, and they let the Hero operate without fingers.

The initial test was a flop. There was no weight attached, but the Hero could not pull at all.

He felt very depressed. He felt like he had failed, not just himself, but everyone who knew what was going on. The anger and anguish was far too much for him, and he left the machine quickly: saying it hurt him in some way.

He then moved over to free weights. The Hero had been using 10 lbs. weights for years before this, so he had a sense of pride going into the situation, even though the previous use of arms went so horribly.

He was handed 2 lbs. weights. He could not lift them at all. He was destroyed spiritually and emotionally. He could not hold back the tears, and he fell apart. Some people go to the gym and sweat pours over their brow. The Hero left with tears pouring off his eyelashes.

Embarrassed, he rolled his large chair to the hall. At least there, he could be out of the eyes of everyone. At least out there, he could look out a window and fantasize about running into the horizon.

He hated this. He hated all of this. Why him? When will it end? He was lost into his head. He had spent so much time in his brain, he almost forgot how to express himself externally. A whirlwind of self-pity and self-loathing, the Hero thought about killing himself for the first time since he got to Hamilton. He could not even see straight. Everything went black.

The Hero did not remember getting back to his room. He was even back in bed which could not have happened without him knowing, could it? Paul was still out of the room. The Hero was confused and just wanted to ask someone what happened.

Just then, a nurse came in to check in on him.

"You're awake! How do you feel?" She asked, breathing a sigh of relief.

It turns out that the Hero had passed out. He was found by the therapists and they had directed his chair back to his room several hours prior. It was now after seven, and dinner was wrapping up soon. She joked about him making an interesting impression on his first full day.

He started crying again and nurse had nothing but sympathy in her eyes. That made everything worse for the Hero. He did not want pity. He did not want people to have to micromanage his life.

Realistically, he was unaware of the months between November and March. He just had other people's stories to go off of. He could recall parts of things, but everything was so surreal that he had no clue what happened. As horribly bored as he was for months, he did not retain much of it. This means that he was not the slightest bit adjusted to the whole situation. He had heard what happened, kind of. There was still a part of him that was expecting to wake up and walk out of the room. He had all but convinced himself that this was all just a horrible dream. He still could not feel his legs at all, and his arms were still rather pathetic.

These facts, and the fact that this cannot be his reality, helped prove the nightmare concept that the Hero came up with.

He pulled himself together. The nurse was saying something about how she understands, but he has to be strong.

The fact of the matter is that you will never understand. No one will.

She was right about one thing, however. He needed to be strong. He straightened up and cleared the tears from his face. Just moments later, Paul came back in the room. He had been down getting dinner and was mildly curious where the Hero had run off to. Apparently, no one had informed him that the Hero passed out earlier.

"It was 'kind-of-chicken' and carrots!" Exclaimed Paul, actually making the air quotes to emphasize that is was horrible. "You missed out on a delicacy!"

The nurse made sure the Hero was okay, checked his vitals, then left the room. Paul shuffled back into his bed and turned on his TV.

What a bizarre Tuesday... thought the Hero. He then put his head back on the pillow and started to dream.

***

Dragons.

Dragons everywhere.

The knight was tasked with the mission of killing every single one of them. Cue bad-nineties action movie themes: the knight rode towards the crowd of snarling teeth and fire on his horse, sword drawn. Sweat beaded down his face and forced his shirt to stick to his torso. The horse kept a steady beat, though it was very apparent to the knight that he was hesitant.

Now, within striking range, the knight let out a mighty battle-cry as he brought his sword down on the head of the first scaled beast. Blood and flames sprayed across the valley they were fighting in. The first dragon fell with a mighty thump. Mighty enough to attract the attention of several more that immediately started to move towards the knight—

The nurse comes in again. So much for the ending of that battle. Paul was awake and up already. The Hero was informed that breakfast and coffee were on the way. The Hero shuddered at the thought of the black paint they passed off as coffee. Paul piped up suddenly.

"He doesn't need a coffee. Mary's got 'im"

Confused, the Hero just accepted and placed his "order" for the rest of the meal. He really hoped that Paul was telling the truth. It was very hard for him these days to function without coffee.

Mary came in baring the black bean juice. This was the greatest moment that the Hero could remember. He sat up in bed, said thank you and drank a good portion of it very quickly. Mary and Paul laughed at him.

Mary was a lovely woman. Hair to her shoulders, soft expression and tall compared to the Hero. It was clear that she loved Paul and that Paul loved her. They explained how they had been together for a long time. Mary was a cancer survivor. Her story was full of depressing anecdotes and horrible experiences.

Paul had nothing but hilarious tales. It was a strange juxtaposition, the Hero thought. It was almost like it was meant to be.

It was almost like it had to be.

7

The Hero still did not know what happened. The last six months were a blur for him. He still had no recollection from November through all of December. He could only remember half of October.

Every day, he was told something else about what had happened. It was beyond the point of mattering, really. He was to be left in a mild fog for the remainder of his journey and, to be honest, it was quite empowering to him.

This is not to say it did not matter: it still weighed heavily on his mind. It was more he had survived what he had to, now he had to find some sort of normality.

He had fallen to prey to what is called "hospitalization." The idea was that time had lost its meaning due to being months in four walls where he was dictated what to do and when. He had also lost all the respect for death he had once had. He watched people give up all hope and resign themselves to a fate that would leave them nothing but a husk of the being that they had once been. He had watched people refuse to accept the hand that had been dealt to them.

At this point, he was happy to have his voice back. The Hero had most of his wits about him. All of these things were never supposed to come back to him. He just had to keep surviving.

April was strange for the Hero. Paul, who he had spent

a month talking to, was coming up to his release back into society. This meant that he would get a new roommate and would have someone new to commiserate with.

Over the last month, he and Paul had created a bond. Not because they were both suddenly bound to wheelchairs, but because they could see the hilarity in the system. They both got through the day by making fun of everything around them. They even made fun of each other's shortcomings. Paul treated the Hero like a son as well as a best friend, and the Hero treated him with nothing but respect and reverence.

The Hero had regained his arm movement in the first week in Hamilton. He was not sure whether it was because of something they did, or it was just time. Regardless, he was ecstatic. They now had him lifting weights in the gym. Though his hands were still somewhat shit, he would lift more and more every week. He was up to 10lbs free weight and 80lbs on a machine.

The machine was a large square structure with four different stations on it, all specific to different muscle groups. The main one that the Hero liked was a collection of weights attached to a rope which went through a pulley. It was the station that had ruined him on his first day, but he was determined to conquer it. The muscles the machine was made to maintain was the scapularies, which are the muscles in the back that govern bicep motion.

A fantastic side effect, the Hero thought, was that the machine would also affect pectoral muscles.

He had always been a well-toned gentleman: he had played drums for over twenty years. He had never put so much focus on his muscles before, however. Everything he had prior was subsequent to what he did. He never worked on anything. He liked the results he was having now.

Occupational therapy was very dry and hard to get through. The Hero's hands had come along very well, so he got very little out of the "class". He could see its importance, however. He saw the importance out in "normal society," making sure houses and whatnot were set up properly for people who may not have been home for months and definitely not in the condition they were in when they left.

His views and general opinions did not change the fact that he was bored for that hour. The most exciting thing he had done in a month was put screws into a board and take them out again.

The Hero was getting annoyed.

One class, they therapist had told him to circle two balls roughly the size of golf balls in one hand. The Hero looked at her and retaliated.

"Can you do that?" He tried to keep his face and tone as polite as he could.

"I… Uh.. Let's find out!" She replied.

She tried for a few minutes. The balls dropped on every rotation she attempted. Frustrated. Defeated. She gave up.

"Yeah. I get it. I can't do it, but you have to." She screamed at the Hero. The therapist then scurried across the room and busied herself in someone else's business.

It was a small victory, but a victory none the less. Proud, the Hero continued to put a screw into a board. Then he screwed it back out. Then he screwed another one back in. Then he took that one back out…

Finally, the hour was up. The Hero put his chair into the fastest it could go and ventured towards the elevator to go outside. This was the first day that was actually good enough to wear a t-shirt in, and the Hero was excited to feel the fresh air.

The sun was pushing hard into the courtyard. There were several small trees that lined the pathway, and the entire face of the building was covered in windows that would never open. The day was particularly quiet, the Hero thought. He slowed his chair down and found a sunny place to park. There, he sat for many hours, lost deep in the recesses of his mind. For once, he was not being reminded of his near-death. For once, he could not compare himself to those who walked. He closed his eyes and drifted with the sounds of the wind and the birds.

***

This one morning was especially fantastic. The sun beamed across the room the Hero was in, his mother came in early, and breakfast was especially fantastic this morning. Even the coffee, or what they called coffee, was manageable.

A collection of hospital staff then came into his room. Confused, the Hero tried to make himself as presentable as possible. The Hero's mother ran to the edge of the room as everyone crammed into the room. It was sudden, and the Hero felt scared.

It was time for a status report, apparently. A bit of warning would have let the Hero be a bit more prepared, but he was not angry. Just a bit dishevelled.

The sun poured into the room as the figures tried to squeeze in as best as they could.

One by one, the different figures expressed how great his advancements were. They were both surprised and excited that he had regained his arm movements so quickly, and they thought his speaking was coming along fantastically.

Then, a woman with strange hair spoke up:

"It's great that you have made such strides, but you will never walk again. Not independently or with aids. Keep going at this pace, though, and you will surely master the wheelchair!"

He had no clue who she was.

As she spoke, the entire room went very still. The therapists, who stood just out of viewing range from the woman, all had gaping mouths. The Hero's mother did not have words. The Hero was not paying attention to the collective. He imagined, at that moment, that time froze in the entire world.

The Hero learned that she was the main doctor for the wing. She was getting her information from the medical notes on the Hero that were from five months ago.

She could not be right. The Hero thought. He was angry. He was curious if she even knew his name.

As fast as the news was dropped, the team dispersed. They had jobs to get back to, they had things to do, they had stuff and whatnot.

The Hero's mother was left with more questions than answers and the possibility of a very upset son. He was not upset though.

He had only just found out who that was. Why would

he EVER consider what she said to be fact? Under what assumption was she basing this rather bold and offensive "truth" around? There was no follow up: no expressed reason. Everyone was just supposed to hear "you'll never walk again" and just shrug off a bomb like that?

She was not the first doctor to say something so bold and uneducated-seeming. There was a doctor while the Hero was in his coma who proclaimed that if he ever woke up, he would be a vegetable. He had called the Hero's parents irresponsible and selfish for ever considering leaving the Hero alive. Even that doctor had showed more evidence than the bitch who just left. The Hero will never refer to her as anything from now on but the bitch.

The Hero was beside himself with anger. He did not go to any of his therapies that day. He barely stayed in the hospital. He immediately went outside and cried. At first out of depression and fear, then out of absolute frustration and disbelief.

"There was no reason given for that!" The Hero yelled towards his shoes as he almost folded himself in half.

"She's an idiot! I hate this too much for it to be an end!" Now, the Hero was getting angry. So was his mother. She agreed with the Hero, pointing out how no one seemed to agree with her. Apparently, a few of the staff had walked up to her and voiced similar opinions after the meeting.

The Hero, on that day, decided that he had to try harder. Harder than he was before to walk, to prove her wrong.

If this was the case, and he is never to walk again, he wanted to know why. He wanted something more concrete than just "oh, ya know, LAWL."

Yet, the Hero could not shake one fear: what if she was right? What if she did not show information because she assumed that the Hero just knew that he was forever trapped in a chair?

He did not hate the wheelchair: it was a necessary and rather fantastic mode of transportation. The Hero was accustomed to using legs, however. He played drums, walked everywhere, and drove: was all that to stop? Was he to continue life with what he had left, and never do what he used to?

8

Paul had left. He had spent the maximum three months, made great strides, and off he went. Paul's leaving was incredibly underwhelming to the Hero, considering how much Paul meant to him. Really, the Hero was ecstatic that he was at a condition to move forward. He was not recovered, but an end was in sight.

The nurses moved the Hero across the room and brought in a new roommate.

The new gentleman was very friendly, but the Hero found himself avoiding him anyway. There was no reason, the Hero just did not want to get attached to him; to a point where the Hero did not even ask what he was in rehab for.

The pressure wound the Hero has had gotten better, to a point, but the wound team (the designation for wound care specialists) were not satisfied with how the pressure sore had healed. They started a procedure they called "E-Stim" on the Hero.

What E-Stim can do fascinated the Hero. The wound was cleaned, then electrodes were placed into the wound. The constant charge would cause enough damage only to invoke healing. The procedure would happen once a day, and the Hero was forced to lie down for at least an hour during the whole procedure. This fact was annoying and boring.

When they were not doing the procedure, they put a vacuum on the hole. It would suck the dead skin off while giving the wound new air. The major downside of this apparatus was that it was permanently on the Hero. It was loud. It was intrusive.

It was necessary.

Because of increased noise level, the Hero was given his own room. The sound was just too constant for everyone. Including the Hero, to be fair. He could not help but feel like he was being pushed aside. Like he was a nuisance to everyone who had to spend time with him. There were tubes and wires literally everywhere he went. The little beast hummed all through the night and would squeal when something went wrong.

Because of the increased noise level, the nursing staff gave the Hero his own room. He was very excited, but he would be totally isolated from every other patient.

The isolation had its upsides. The Hero was able to watch whatever he wanted at whatever volume he found appropriate. He could have visitors, who were mostly his parents, whenever he wanted and for as long as he wanted. He could lock himself away from the world of doctors and nurses for as long as he wanted and dwell on thoughts of philosophy and logic.

He was fit with a new chair. This one was manual, which made the Hero very happy. It was small, quick, and stealthy. It took the Hero all of an hour to get comfortable in it, and he was off.

There were many obstacles to get used to. Hills and abrupt stops were two things that really pushed the Hero to the limits of his physical ability.

We aren't supposed to use arms as legs. the Hero thought to himself, as the pain settled into his joints.

It was around this time that he met a girl and a boy. The girl had been in a horrific snowmobile accident that broke her spine. The boy had cannonballed into a pool and hit the bottom. The three of them were quick friends.

The boy, being the youngest of the three, was also well versed in being in hospital. This was his second adventure after spending three months in a children's facility in a far- away land. He had many tales of other people he had met, what happened to them, and where they were last he saw them.

The girl was, rightfully, angry. She was far from defeated, to be fair. She was determined in everything she did to perfect it. She had the demeanour, the Hero felt, that she had been in a chair her entire life. This was in spite of the fact that he knew it had only been a few months.

The three of them were awkward friends. They would make inappropriate jokes about being in wheelchairs, and they took great pride in making people around them uncomfortable. Together, with another chap a few rooms over from the Hero, they spent all of their time trying to one-up the other.

The boy knew a lot about wheelchairs. He knew what all of the parts were called, brands, what makes that were better than others, and perfect sizes for speed. This surprised the Hero. He had lived most of his life assuming that a wheelchair was a wheelchair. It turns out that there is a whole industry making wheelchairs for whatever walk of life one could imagine. It makes sense, it just is something the Hero had never thought about.

The chair the Hero got for himself was small and green. The Hero liked green. It was not the smallest, but very close. Made for speed, manoeuvrability, and transportation: it was promised to be a fantastic ride.

The Hero felt excited but defeated. Purchasing a wheelchair was almost like accepting that he is where he will be for a very long time. He had nothing wrong with this idea from an external visage, but he wanted to walk. He could not help but feel it was normal, whatever normal was. He had been shown an entire under-appreciated world, and he liked belonging to it. It was something new, something different, and something where there was less unfriendly competition.

The challenge to deal with the world and make everything work. He wanted to get into planning accessibility for the masses. He wanted to make sure everything was able to be worked by everyone. From doors to ramp angles. The Hero felt himself compelled to help people with questions they may have.

9

The Hero was having issues seeing. Everything was bouncing, and he could not focus. He would start to read a line, and it would bleed into the line below it. Everything was kind of blurry. This was not new.

The Hero just assumed it was "normal." He had seen several eye specialists, and they all said the same thing: "Your eyes are fine. Better than fine."

Of course, leave it to having a brain issue to make people notice. He was forwarded to an Ophthalmologist when he complained one day. It was at a hospital across town, so his mother and brother came to take him.

They were healthy when they first came down.

The drive was dystopian and strange. The journey took them through an industrial sector, and it looked abandoned.

Everywhere the Hero looked, there were smokestacks and broken windows. The factories all looked to be abandoned, even though they probably were not. No one was on the sidewalks, and the road was full of industrial traffic going from one abandoned building to another. The air was thick and yellow with smog and tar.

Rain finally broke as they came up to the front doors. A thunderstorm had rolled in. The Hero could only laugh at how fitting the dark skies were against the large brick and metal buildings. The rain quickly cleared up a good portion of the air, and it really struck the Hero how horrible the condition of the atmosphere was in this neighbourhood.

The doors were the standard double-sliding doors that were on most hospitals. The air was the standard recycled air that was in most hospitals. These were things that should not have been so apparent to the Hero.

He was becoming accustomed to the feel of hospitals.

They checked in at the admitting desk and found a place to park the Hero. The waiting room was mostly empty: only a few people were taking up the seating, and they were all older.

The Hero was actually nervous for the first time in his journey. He would be introduced by his name, case, and medical history. He would not be able to express who he was. He was a number on a chart.

Finally, his name was called. All in all, they waited just a few moments. His mother and brother joined him for the assessment.

The first doctor was very friendly, yet still professional. He started asking the Hero questions about him, not about his medical history. He got the Hero to read letters from the wall, all while he was making notes on a pad of paper. He was a student doing an internship.

In walked the surgeon. He came off as cold and uncaring, the Hero thought. He did not even do very many tests, he just seemed concerned with what the student wrote.

"It sounds like an astigmatism. We will have to do brain surgery." He proclaimed. He sounded very proud of his assessment.

The Hero was beside himself. He had literally gone from "your eyes are great" to "you need to put your life in my hands" in a matter of moments. He was sceptical. How dare someone who did nothing proclaim something so invasive. How dare he.

The Hero remained polite on the outside. He simply smiled and said "okay" then continued to sit through the interaction. He was steaming. He could see his mother out of the corner of his eye, and she was visibly upset. The Hero knew the look she had on her face. Her eyes were narrow, her brow furrowed. The Hero could tell she was being polite but holding in a rage that would be unmatched. They both seemed to be in agreement that this was bold, to say the least. Then the interaction was over.

Brain surgery? The Hero was very sceptical. He wanted a second opinion from someone who would give him the time of day, from someone who actually tried to rule that out. No advancements were made that day.

The Hero, his brother, and his mother then all piled into the car. There had been an awkward silence leading up to that point. The kind of silence that seemed forced, the kind of silence that one could cut with a knife. Then, the Hero's brother spoke up.

"So, does anyone else see that as a giant waste of time?"

There was a feeling of relief that someone said it. The Hero's mother laughed and the two of them talked about how ridiculous that whole altercation was. They were only at the hospital for an hour and then brain surgery was the only option.

They made the drive back through the industrial graveyard, then found a parking spot back at the hospital. The Hero's brother then complained about his throat being hoarse, and the Hero's mother felt lethargic and drained.

Yay, Hamilton.

Back at his room, his haven, the Hero loaded up the

laptop that he had. He wanted to write horrible things. He wanted to rant and rave. He wanted to never see another "specialist" as long as he lived. Instead, he watched a funny video on the internet of cats being jerks and went to bed.

The next day, the Hero was asked by one of the nurses about his appointment. He was as polite as he could be, only expressing the event as interesting. He put on the most genuine smile he could about the whole thing. The nurse from the back of the room saw through the facade right away.

"Waste of time?" She asked in a very dry tone.

The Hero did not respond to this. He just continued the half-smile and rolled into the hall. He wanted someone to help him. He wanted some sort of solace. He wanted an adhesive medical strip to get him to the next hurdle.

"Maybe," he thought. "everything will get better."

He did not want to talk about the appointment. If it was true, he still wanted a second opinion. He wanted someone to see him as human: as a person. Was this selfish? Was this too much to ask from the medical "community"?

"Community." That was something to laugh about. Nurses and therapists showed true aspirations to make their patients feel like individuals. Doctors and surgeons, from the Hero's perspective, just wanted to get through their day.

He does not blame them: there job is full of bad news and guesses. This, in turn, puts them in a position to get yelled at, often. The Hero did not make a fuss, he was still too angry and depressed to do so.

The next week for the Hero was very hard to get through. He knew it was just one opinion, but the idea that he might need yet another brain surgery was daunting. From the way the surgeon was talking, it was permanent. There was no way to make it better, and even surgery was not a guaranteed thing. *My eyes were no worse than they used to be*, he thought. *What has changed now?*

That is when he found out something that sounded rather "cool" to the Hero. When he was close to death at the beginning of this journey, his right eye had succumbed to major damage. The build-up of pressure against his optical nerve had caused his eye to "explode". His pupil had become square, like a goat, and the iris had become non-responsive. There was a lot of concern that he would never be able to see from that eye again. It had fully healed physically in just over a month, so the concern dissipated.

The Hero was rather intrigued by this prospect. He also wondered why it took him six months to hear about this. The fact now gave credence to what the surgeon said, not that he was sold on the idea of brain surgery.

Back to what he needed to do. Adventure over. Time does not stop in the face of revelation. The Hero knew this too well.

10

The last month was a bit strange. The Hero could barely figure out what happened, and he had no idea what would be next. All he knew was that he had to keep going. He had to keep progressing. No amount of preparing could have made him ready for this particular morning.

He had been without connection to the outside world for seven months at this point. The Hero felt isolated and rejected for this entire time. His only saving grace had been Paul, his family, and the few friends he had been in contact with. Even his work had been out of contact with the Hero since the beginning of the event in November. This gave the Hero the chance he craved to find himself again: to find something that he felt he had lost. A sense of individuality and strength that he had not felt for years prior to the coma. Finally, he thought it would be a good idea to look to see what his friends had said on social media.

That was a horrible idea.

Two pages of farewells. Two. They were personal, loving, and misinformed.

From what the Hero could read, word got out that he had died. It is the only explanation for his disappearance, according to the masses. There was nothing about what he had gone through. There was nothing about how he was. There was nothing about what was next.

He wept. For the first time, he felt like he had made an impact on people and that he was actually missed.

After the tears had finally gone away, the Hero realized how morbid this whole event was. He was reading a kind of obituary. He was looking at what people had to say and how they wanted to say it. They were voicing things assuming that he would never see or read it. Expressions of frustration and greed were mixed in with sentiments of horror and empathy. It felt, to him, like people were competing to say they were more upset by the event.

The Hero was torn. Did he delete his accounts online and do a true digital death? This would allow him to start again. This would mean that no one could find him. Even if he started a new account, they would assume it was someone else or fake.

Would he post something sentimental and loving? Would he appease everyone with love and well-wishes?

Nope.

"Alive and kicking in Hamilton."

The Hero smiled to himself as he hit the submit button. He knew what the reaction of those who were unaware of what has happened would be. He knew that it was gentle enough that those who knew what was going on would just smirk.

He would not respond to anything posted on his update. Laughing, he simply put his laptop away and stared out at the beautiful spring day that was going on outside.

Even if he was indeed dead, life goes on. He understood the need to mourn, as he had a few of his close friends unfortunately die in this rat race that is life. He wondered how seeing his obituary would affect his mindset. Nobel read his obituary and started the Nobel Peace Prize to change public opinion. Would he become the person everyone said he was, or was that truly who he was?

Never to use a walker or any other assistive devices. They said he would never stand again. They said that he could do nothing to move forward.

These are things that the Hero kept reminding himself of. Not as a reason to not try, quite the opposite. These were proclamations that drove him to try even harder. He wanted the medical world to shrivel in embarrassment. He wanted to prove everyone wrong.

It had become almost like a kind of challenge: see how far one can get when there is supposedly no chance for recovery.

Today would be the day. Today, he would go onto a walker. Today, he would leave the world of wheelchairs behind.

First step: standing up. Easy, even for the Hero. Second step: taking a step. Also easy.

Third step: continue taking steps.

The third step proved itself to be more difficult than the Hero expected. He got dizzy. Not in the traditional world spinning kind of way, but more of a full body exhaustion kind of way. He could only manage a few inches before he had to sit down on his wheelchair again.

Were they right? What was going wrong? Why could he not do this? The Hero erupted into tears. He did not care who saw.

These were not tears of depression or defeat, but of determination and confusion. Not even he could understand why he could not do it: what muscles were not activating to make this so hard. He had legs. He could feel. He even had most, if not all, muscle control.

I know. I'll just try again. He thought to himself. He was determined to push through the pain and fatigue. He could do this! He knew he could! *At least ten steps!*

He succeeded at failing, at the cost of any happiness he had left. He was sore. He was tired.

The Hero, defeated, only uttered one phrase under his breath. "She was right."

The Hero was done for the day. His legs were shaking with the pain. His vision had started to blur. He wanted to throw in the towel.

He would try every day for the next year. He got further some days, and some days he was too tired to get to a halfway point.

11

The Hero was getting used to uprooting his life every couple of weeks. He got to stay in his own room for about four weeks before being moved to another floor. It was either that or kick him out of hospital.

The Hero was getting very good at moving. Mind you, he did not have much to pack: just a few pairs of pants, a few shirts, his phone and his laptop. The nurses still had to help him, even though he was just moving one floor. This was quite the intimidating experience for the Hero. He had made friends! He had a routine! Now, he would have to start all over.

In the other room, he had a roommate again. He was a nice fellow, about four years younger than the Hero. He was in a car accident and had smashed his head into something. It ruined his ability to interact, but he was still a very nice fellow.

The floor they moved him to was the Acquired Brain Injury wing: also known as the ABI Wing. It was for situations where the cognitive functions took a harder hit than any other part of the body.

It was only one floor away from where the Hero resided initially, but it was a very different world. They went about everything very differently. For one: the physical therapy was almost non-existent and focused on different things aside from where the Hero struggled. There was, for good reason, more emphasis put on brain activity and things of that nature.

The Hero felt like he did not belong. He made friends fast enough, but he always had this nagging feeling that he should not be there.

The main reason they moved him upstairs was because he would be able to continue physiotherapy at the same times and with the same people that he had become used to over the last couple of months. This meant that, twice a day, he would get to go back to the floor he missed and interact with people he knew.

The Hero could even admit that the ABI wing was not without its merit. There was a very nice square-shaped garden in the middle of the ward. They were on a locked ward, which meant that there was a passcode to use the doors to get in and out. This caused them not to have the same access to the outside that floor two had. As isolating as it sounded, the result was an increased feeling of security.

The garden and seating area were beautiful. It was right in the centre of the ward. All of the halls that had a view to it were covered in floor to ceiling windows. If there was a room between the hall and the view, that room would have windows. There were only a couple of blind spots. They were rooms for staff, or they were storage rooms.

The biggest downside to this garden oasis was its proximity to an emergency helipad. There would be hours upon hours of silence, then, the roar of an engine coupled with the swoosh of spinning blades would interrupt. Conversation would have to crawl, if not stop, during this time period. The Hero definitely understood the importance of these metal birds, but he still hated them. The bright orange would reflect the light and blind those on the ground. The weather would actually be affected by their ignition.

Seriously, the Hero recognized the importance of the helicopters.

12

Today was the day.

Today, the Hero would be leaving Hamilton for a while. A part of him was sad to have it going behind him. It had been his home for four months. It was the longest he had stayed somewhere that was not his parents' house.

He had independence, even if it was just an illusion.

He would be going back to Freeport in Kitchener. His parents were not ready for him to go back home. His house was far from accessible. He did not even have a toilet that he could use.

So, off to Freeport he went. The hospital ordered him a Patient Transfer vehicle to take him there. The upside of this was that he could stay in his chair for the trip. The downside was that he would be alone with the driver.

To the Hero's relief, the driver was friendly. He was an older gentleman, about sixty. Except to help to get the Hero in the vehicle, he was not intrusive in any way. The Hero was not troubled by the music he was playing, either. It was your standard top forty junk. The kind of sound that just filled the air, was incredibly forgettable, and soothed the minds of millions.

About halfway through the trip, the Hero was given quite the fright.

"You know where we are going, right? You have been there before?" The driver asked, expecting a quick response.

Yes, the Hero had been there before. He was lying down, counting the seconds between each breath. Then, his stretcher was pulled out of the back of the van and he was whisked inside.

Does he know where he was going? Hell no. He was not even sure what day it was.

He relayed this information to the driver, who looked incredibly distraught over the information he was given.

The Hero knew ROUGHLY where they were going. He could get them, comfortably, within five kilometres of where they needed to be.

"That would not be enough," said the driver.

The Hero and the driver found the right area. Luckily, for both of them, there was a car dealership that was open close to where they were going. The driver ran in to ask directions while the Hero waited in his chair.

Now, the music was getting on the Hero's nerves. Every song sounded the same to him. Every beat, every strum, every vocal melody. It had been eight months that he was out of the music industry. He feared that this is where music was going.

Then, the Hero started to laugh. Very hard, too hard. It was borderline manic: tears were flowing from his eyes and he could not catch his breath.

"I spend eight months in hospitals, and this is what I worry about?" He thought to himself. It was, at that moment, that he would stop worrying about the way he was supposed to be. Nothing had changed in his brain. He was still the music-obsessed slacker that he has always been.

It was at that time that the driver came back to the vehicle: happy and glowing.

"It's fuckin' next door!" He exclaimed excitedly. They then pulled away from the doors of the dealership and continued their journey. The driver never noticed the state the Hero was in. He did not have to see a reflection to know that he looked dishevelled. The mostly-healed hole in his neck framed by his beard that was undoubtably starting to grow back.

They took the small detour they needed to take and started the drive up to the front of the large building. It was spring. There were flowers everywhere around the facility, but no people were to be seen. Then, just as the Hero was about to point out how surreal the situation was, he could make out the silhouette of his mother and brother walking up the hill to the entrance.

Back to the mansion. The air was much cleaner, the view was nicer, the people were friendlier. He had a great time in Hamilton, but it was nice to be close to what he knows. What he knew.

It was surprising to him that there were a few people who remembered the Hero. He thought it was Province-wide that you had to leave rehab after three months regardless of condition, but he was happy there were people who remembered him. It created a sense of camaraderie.

The Hero was at a loss, however. The last time he had been there, he was a husk. He was unable to speak when he first entered, and barely whispered when he left. He could not move one finger before. Now, he was able to move his whole body to his knees.

A Physiotherapy assistant met him in his room when the reintroductions were over and the Hero was alone.

"You have improved greatly since the last time you were here." he stated, almost bashfully. The Hero wondered where he was going with this thought. It seemed like an awkward place to stop, and his tone lead itself perfectly to a continuation.

"We assumed you would be brain dead or just fully dead. We definitely did not expect you so vibrant and well!"

This was meant as a compliment, but it cut the Hero deep. Dead? In every sense of the word, he was far from dead. The Hell he had been through over the last eight months... the memories he had retained.

He was not dead.

There was not anything more said between the two of them that day. The Hero was rather astonished that he was living yet another "return from the grave" and he was not overly thrilled about it.

He shared a room with three other men. They were very friendly, but there was definitely a generation gap. The Hero just stayed in his corner of the room whenever he was forced to stick around that area. It was dim, but he was segregated from the rest of the people. It was his oasis: his place to read, write, and think.

They put him back in physiotherapy and occupational therapy. Physiotherapy continued to work on things like weight training and walking, whereas occupational therapy focused more on the psychological aspects.

There was still no diagnosis.

Food was better. The Hero learned how to properly

pivot transfer (the act of moving from one stationary seat to another without any aids). He continued to do his best. What made it easier was the better food, better air, and better friends.

At the Hero's table, there was Mary and Mary. In writing, it looks confusing, but it made everything so much easier. Especially because they were such different people.

Mary had an aneurysm, which destroyed her memory and changed who she was.

Mary had a stroke. It left her paralyzed on one side.

The one thing they had in common was that they both loved to talk. This was not a bad thing for the Hero: they would fill him in about happenings around the building, sports, news, and family. It was a nice change from the silence that he had crafted for himself.

The other fantastic thing about being back in town was that friends could come and see him much more often. Since he had access to the outside world again, people knew where he was. They knew how to get a hold of him. There would never be a chain of people telling other people to tell people to come out. All this and he had a fantastic court he could go out into. It was open to the sun, the wind was mostly blocked by the buildings, and there were trees everywhere.

Occupational therapy time. His least favourite time. The Therapist went on tangents talking to herself and would relay what she thought was a good idea occasionally to the Hero. It is not that she was totally off base with everything she said, but she would not listen. She would only take in what she wanted to hear and ignore everything else. This includes if the everything else dealt with over-taxing or pain.

Her main concern seemed to be the Hero's eyes. He had not done any additional tests since he was told that he needed brain surgery, but he wanted to know that he would be fine. The therapist wrote up a referral to a place a city over. It was a teaching facility. The important thing about this place was that they were prone to doing important work in the name of science.

13

He was coming along swimmingly: The Hero had gained back the use of 95% of his body, but the end was nowhere in sight. There was one issue. The Hero still could not walk. Furthermore, why would he go through periods of extreme exhaustion that would seemingly come out of nowhere? His bladder also seemed to be working incorrectly, but that was more annoying than an issue.

He could not keep his balance when he tried. His back and shoulders would seize up when he used either a cane or a walker. He kept locking his legs whenever he did stand, which is not what our bodies were made to do with any sort of regularity.

The sudden fatigue thing was very concerning to the hero, but it was always pushed to the background as he was made to focus on walking. Secretly, he found it far more pressing than he let on. The sudden feeling of exhaustion followed by very heavy limbs did not really impact him while he was in hospital: he felt if there was an actual issue, it would have been noticed by medical personnel. No one said anything, so he should just not worry. Was that the correct path to take?

The Hero found the few physical deformities very frustrating. He could not figure out what was wrong, and no one would tell him. Was it a balance or a muscle thing? Was the sudden fatigue a brain thing, or a healing thing?

Would he ever recover?

Some doctors say no, but they never say why. He needed a why. He really needed to know if he was going to recover, or if he was wasting his time. It would not stop him completely, but the Hero would be less hard on himself if he knew it was an uphill battle.

Things in the hospital were getting awkward, and the Hero was left only to fear the worst. It was not the horrible, unbearable kind of awkward. It was more the "I know something you don't and I'm sorry" kind of awkward.

The Hero got to find out what it was.

He was summoned to a meeting. He did not understand what was going on, but the head of the facility was there, and several other people he had never met before. Also in the company were both his parents, the Therapists, and his social worker. They all started talking about how the Hero had surpassed what they could do. He was to be thrown out.

His Father weighed in. He claimed that their house was not suitable for the Hero. He claimed that it would be detrimental to both the Hero and the family if they had to have him back home already.

The hospital folded their arms: their position was final. The Hero was to leave in a weeks' time.

The Hero was actually elated about the decision. His Father doubted his ability, and everyone else thought that he was hopeless, but he knew he could do this. He knew that being released into the world was the best thing that could happen at this time. He would learn to adapt to a world not made for people in wheelchairs. He would become everything no one thought he would ever become. He was sure of it. Would the road ahead be very hard work? He would have to be stupid to think it would not be. Was he nervous? Absolutely. The only way left to progress would be to travel at his own pace and do what was never expected.

He feared that he was being arrogant. Maybe he would relapse and fall back to a helpless state. There was little to no attention being placed on the incredible fatigue or his bladder. The Hero could not blame anyone, for he put little emphasis on how concerned he was, as well.

Regardless of the outcome, and the feelings of those around him, he was excited to leave institutions behind. At least, on the permanent level. He was aware that he would have to return every few days for therapy. He assumed that he would need more frequent check-ups to make sure he was still in a good state. He knew that his mental state was the same as always: bleak, but hopeful. There was a bit of him that was concerned that the freedom would overwhelm him and his metal state would deteriorate, but it was a situation that the Hero would face head-on.

The best way to define the way he felt was "Fuck It." A year ago, he would not even imagine being in a wheelchair, and now he was being told that he would never be out of one. A year ago, he would never sleep, rarely eat, and worked far too much. Now, he had not been employed in a year, could not go eight hours without a meal, and needed to nap halfway through the day and needed to sleep at nine.

Maybe his New Normal was what he needed? Maybe, just maybe, he could do this.

Fuck maybe.

He HAD to do this. If he did nothing, he would die. If he gave in, he may as well die.

Well, die again.

Still, he had gone too far. He had put up with enough. He had this feeling that people were looking to see what he does next. It was clear that the masses were interested in what he was doing: that was evident by the barrage of questions he got on a regular basis. Yes, his family was scared, but so was he. His friends seemed like they were trying too hard not to offend him. He would mock them to their faces. Society would go out of its way to make sure it is being "politically correct". He would go out of his way to show how backwards things could be.

He now had plans! The Hero is positive that reality will set in and everything will go to Hell, but plans: he sure did have some! He spent the next few hours poring over laws and regulations. He polled his contacts about how they would act in certain situations involving a person in a wheelchair. There was a direction somewhere in these actions, he was sure of it!

Then, like the world knew he was doing things that would disturb it, he collapsed onto the keyboard of his laptop. The Hero was out until his parents came later that night to pick him up to take him away from hospitals forever.

14

The final release home was a joyous event. The first week was a parade of people coming around. Some of those people had not seen the Hero for months, and they were quite happy with how far he had come.

The departure from institutions was much needed: every day was a routine, and every day was the same. It drove the Hero completely insane. The feeling of wasting away was becoming apparent. He knows that everyone was just trying to help in some way, but he missed his independence. He missed the freedom that came with his previous life.

He still lived at his parents' house, and probably will for a very long time. The idea crushed the Hero. Gone were the days of just getting in the vehicle and driving to wherever and just worrying if the gas tank had enough fuel to get him home. Gone were the days of recording albums, performing on stage, and doing what he wanted.

Were they gone forever?

This was a chance to start over. This was the second chance to be the person that everyone thought he was. He had tried the independent music scene for over ten years, maybe it was about time he tried something new.

Chrissy and her boy, Adam, were as close as ever to the Hero. They made the trek to visit him as often as they could, always with open arms and excitement to try new things.

The Hero started a blog to try to answer the questions that everyone had. It was easier to direct the masses to a source as opposed to trying to answer the same questions over and over and over...

In May of 2015, the Hero assisted his good friend Katie in bringing her art to the masses. Her and the Hero met in early 2010 when she did some photography work for a band that he was in. Katie went to concerts very often and ran a publication to demonstrate her photography prowess. The Hero opened a website for her and started writing a music review article every week. Her reader count had more than doubled in one year.

He did actually try going to school. He tried very hard. The first program he enrolled in was a bit of a wash. The material was too difficult to do from a wheelchair. Disheartened, he tried his hand at computer programming. That seemed to go a lot better for a little bit.

What is he doing next?

Even he is not sure. He is just going about his days and trying to figure out how to live being in a wheelchair for now. He has no doubts that he will walk again one day: he is also aware that not adapting to his current and new existence will lead to tears. He still gets up to walk at least three times a week.

He wants to live a life that works. He no longer wants to be the burden he assumes he is.

At least he's not dead.

Life continues for the Hero. He met the love of his life, Natasha. After just shy of two years, they wed. It was a very small ceremony, only involving family and a couple of friends. The Hero would not have asked for the ceremony to be another way. They moved to a nearby city to start anew. Life looked grand and hopeful for the Hero for the first time in a very long time.

That was short lived, however. Very short lived.

They married on the 14th of July, and he was diagnosed epileptic by the first of August after he fell from his chair and was rushed to hospital on a stretcher. This explained why he had such a hard time with school. This explains the incredible fatigue he would feel randomly. Natasha swore that she loved him regardless, but he was worried that he was becoming the burden that he swore he would never be again.

There would be a cavalcade of doctor visits and specialists that came with the diagnosis of epilepsy. The Hero was confounded that after almost a year in hospital, no one noticed that this was a thing. The safety risk alone should have made that a priority over everything else he was faced with.

Slowly, things started to make sense. He was put on an hour of bedrest a day since at the Hamilton hospital. He was never given a clear reason why, but now he assumed that it was because of the seizures. He had failed classes that he found very easy while he was in college. Was it because he was missing something fundamental? Or was it because he was missing half the lesson due to losing consciousness randomly?

Conversations ending abruptly, lapses in memory... all of these things were now viewed by the Hero in a different lens. He used to worry it was just him being forgetful, but really it was beyond any control he could